Smithsonian

LITTLE EXPLORER

SPACE FLIGHTS

by Kathryn Clay

CAPSTONE PRESS
a capstone imprint

Little Explorer is published by Capstone Press
1710 Roe Crest Drive, North Mankato, Minnesota 56003

www.mycapstone.com

Library of Congress Cataloging-in-Publication Data
Names: Clay, Kathryn, author.
Title: Space flights / by Kathryn Clay.
Description: North Mankato, Minnesota : Capstone Press, [2017]
| Series: Smithsonian little explorer. Little astronauts | Audience:
Ages 7–9. | Audience: K to grade 3. | Includes bibliographical
references and index.
Identifiers: LCCN 2016043030| ISBN 9781515736592 (library
binding) | ISBN 9781515736738 (pbk.) | ISBN 9781515736776
(ebook (pdf))
Subjects: LCSH: Manned space flight—Juvenile literature. |
Manned space flight—History—Juvenile literature. | Outer
space—Exploration—Juvenile literature.
Classification: LCC TL793 .C6268 2017 | DDC 629.45—dc23
LC record available at https://lccn.loc.gov/2016043030

Editorial Credits

Arnold Ringstad, editor; Laura Polzin, designer and production
specialist

Our very special thanks to Dr. Valerie Neal, Curator and Chair
of the Space History Department at the Smithsonian National
Air and Space Museum for her curatorial review. Capstone
would also like to thank Kealy Gordon, Smithsonian Institution
Product Development Manager, and the following at Smithsonian
Enterprises: Christopher A. Liedel, President; Carol LeBlanc,
Senior Vice President; Brigid Ferraro, Vice President; Ellen
Nanney, Licensing Manager.

Photo Credits

Getty Images: Hulton Archives/Keystone, 19, UIG/Sovfoto, 18,
26; NASA: cover, 1, 3, 6 (background), 6 (foreground), 7, 8, 9 (left),
9 (right), 13, 14, 15 (bottom), 16 (background), 16 (foreground), 17,
20, 21, 23, 25 (top), 25 (bottom), 27, 28, 29 (top), 29 (bottom), 30–31;
Science Source, 4, 24, RIA Novosti, 5 (top), 10, 11, 12; Shutterstock:
pockygallery, 15 (top)

Design Elements: Shutterstock Images: Antares_StarExplorer,
MarcelClemens, Ovchinnkov Vladimir, pio3, Shay Yacobinski,
Tashal, Teneresa

Printed in the United States of America.
062017   010595R

TABLE OF CONTENTS

SPACEX

THE FIRST PERSON IN SPACE

On April 12, 1961, the Soviet Union launched a rocket into space. At the rocket's top was a small spacecraft. Cosmonaut Yuri Gagarin was inside. He became the first person in space.

The Soviet Union later split into several countries, including Russia.

Gagarin's launch

Gagarin was in space for 108 minutes. He circled the planet once. Then he returned to Earth. His mission paved the way for many amazing space flights.

Yuri Gagarin

Astronauts from 40 countries have flown in space.

MAJOR SPACE FLIGHTS

mission name	launch date	accomplishments	country
Vostok 1	April 12, 1961	first person in space	Soviet Union
Gemini 8	March 16, 1966	first docking	United States
Apollo 11	July 16, 1969	first moon landing	United States
Soyuz 11	June 6, 1971	first space station boarding	Soviet Union
STS-1	April 12, 1981	first space shuttle flight	United States
STS-135	July 8, 2011	last space shuttle flight	United States

THE FIRST AMERICAN IN SPACE

NASA soon sent the first U.S. astronaut into space. On May 5, 1961, Astronaut Alan Shepard flew into space in a small capsule. It was called *Freedom 7*.

Alan Shepard

NASA stands for National Aeronautics and Space Administration. It is the United States' space agency.

Shepard did not circle Earth. Instead, he flew up to a height of 116 miles (187 kilometers). He came right back down. His space flight lasted about 15 minutes.

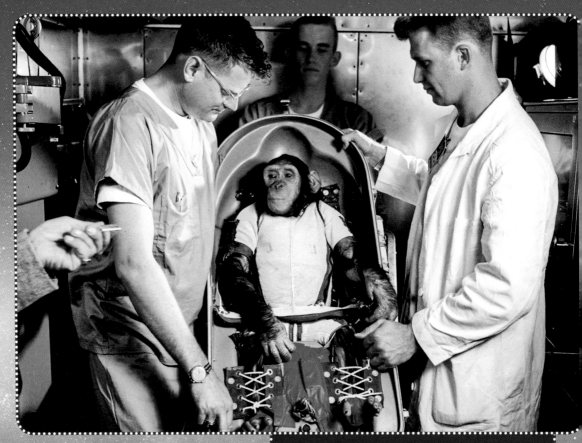

A chimpanzee named Ham flew on the flight before Shepard's mission.

NASA tested its early capsules using chimpanzees.

JOHN GLENN'S HISTORIC FLIGHT

John Glenn became the first American to orbit Earth. His capsule, *Friendship 7*, launched from Florida on February 20, 1962. Glenn circled Earth three times. He spent about five hours in space.

Glenn climbs into his spacecraft.

Glenn was a national hero. People in New York City celebrated his space flight with a parade. Cities named schools and streets after him.

Glenn in 1962

Glenn in 1998

Glenn flew into space again 36 years later. He joined six other astronauts on a winged spacecraft called a space shuttle in 1998. At 77 years old, he was the oldest astronaut ever.

THE FIRST WOMAN IN SPACE

The first woman to fly in space was Valentina Tereshkova. She was an experienced parachutist from the Soviet Union.

Tereshkova (left) had experience parachuting from planes.

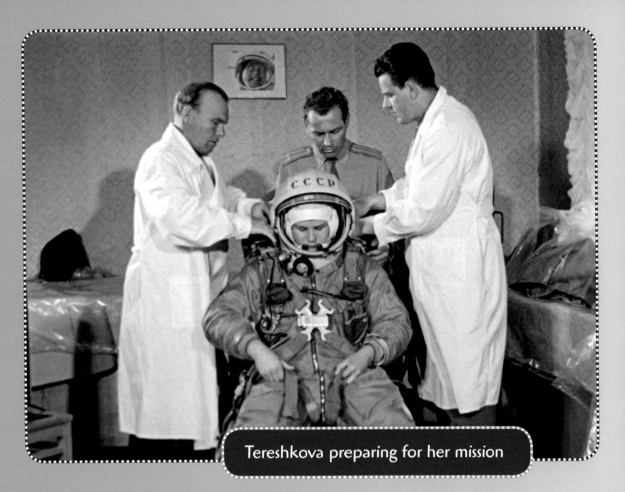

Tereshkova preparing for her mission

Tereshkova flew on the Vostok 6 mission. Her mission began on June 16, 1963. She circled the planet 48 times in nearly 71 hours.

It was 19 years before another woman went into space. Cosmonaut Svetlana Savitskaya flew in August 1982.

Leonov painted this image of his spacewalk.

THE FIRST SPACEWALK

When a person exits a spacecraft in space, it is called a spacewalk. Cosmonaut Alexei Leonov was the first person to go on a spacewalk. On March 18, 1965, he spent 10 minutes floating outside his ship. He stayed connected to the ship by a tether.

A few months later, Ed White became the first U.S. astronaut to go on a spacewalk. He did this on the Gemini 4 mission. White also used a tether so he would not float away from his ship.

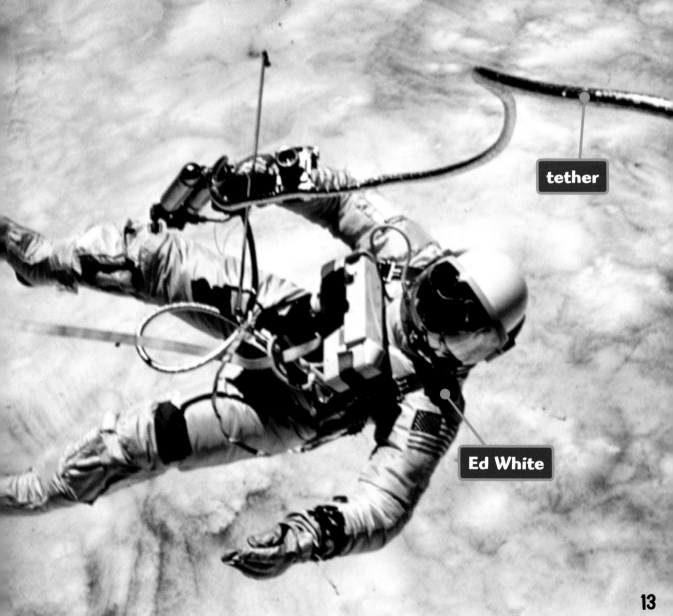

tether

Ed White

ORBITING THE MOON

On December 24, 1968, the Apollo 8 mission orbited the moon. U.S. Astronauts Frank Borman, Jim Lovell, and Bill Anders were onboard. They were the first people to go so far away from Earth. They watched their home planet rise over the moon's horizon. They returned safely to Earth a few days later.

NASA prepared for a moon landing. The astronauts on the Apollo 9 and Apollo 10 missions tested their spacecraft. They practiced the steps they would need to land. They hoped their planning would pay off.

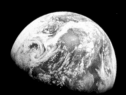

The Apollo 8 astronauts took photos of Earth rising.

APOLLO 8 FLIGHT PATH

(distances not to scale)

LUNAR ORBIT

When a spacecraft is circling the moon, it is said to be in lunar orbit. On the Apollo 8 mission, the astronauts orbited the moon ten times before returning home.

LANDING

LAUNCH

THE MOON LANDING

On July 20, 1969, the three astronauts of the Apollo 11 mission launched to the moon. They were Neil Armstrong, Buzz Aldrin, and Michael Collins.

Apollo 11 lifted off from Florida.

Michael Collins

Buzz Aldrin

Neil Armstrong

Armstrong and Aldrin took the lander down to the moon's surface. Collins waited in the main spacecraft in lunar orbit. Armstrong and Aldrin exited the lander and walked around. They collected rocks and soil to study. They took photos. A few days later, all three men returned to Earth.

lunar module

Buzz Aldrin

The astronauts set up science experiments on the surface of the moon.

THE FIRST SPACE STATION

The Soviet Union launched the first space station on April 19, 1971. It was named Salyut 1. The station did not have anyone traveling inside.

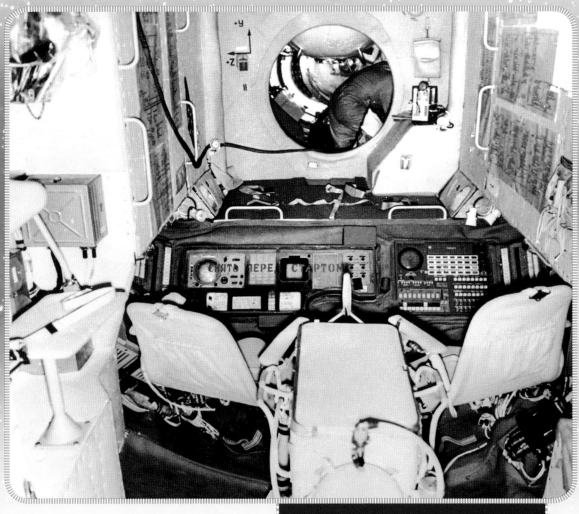

inside the Salyut 1 space station

The crew of the Soyuz 11 mission flew to the station in June 1971. They stayed aboard for 23 days. Sadly all three crew members died. The air leaked out of their spacecraft as they returned to Earth. The cosmonauts didn't have enough oxygen to survive.

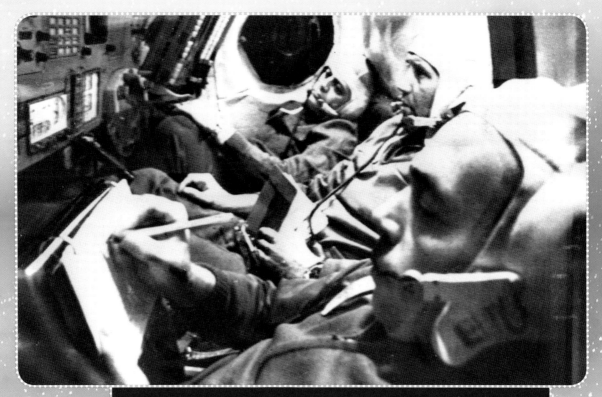

The Soyuz 11 crew included Vladislav Volkov (left), Viktor Patsayev (middle), and Georgi Dobrovolski (right).

INTERNATIONAL SPACE STATION

The largest space station ever built is the International Space Station (ISS). It usually holds six people at a time.

THE SPACE SHUTTLE

The space shuttle was the first reusable spacecraft. It could return to Earth, then be launched into space again. There have been five space shuttles. They were named *Columbia, Challenger, Discovery, Atlantis,* and *Endeavour.*

fuel tank

space shuttle orbiter

solid rocket boosters

USA

The first shuttle launched on April 12, 1981. *Columbia* took off from Florida. Astronauts John Young and Bob Crippen flew the ship. The men circled Earth 36 times. They landed the ship in the California desert like an airplane.

the space shuttle *Columbia* landing

THE FIRST AMERICAN WOMAN IN SPACE

In 1977 Sally Ride answered a newspaper advertisement from NASA. The space agency was looking for more astronauts. About 8,000 people applied. Ride was one of 35 who were chosen.

On June 18, 1983, she became the first American woman in space. Ride flew on the space shuttle *Challenger*. She carried out science experiments in space. She inspired many girls and women.

TIMELINE: WOMEN IN SPACE

1982
Svetlana Savitskaya is the second woman in space.

1984
Svetlana Savitskaya is the first woman to go on a spacewalk.

1963
Valentina Tereshkova becomes the first woman in space.

1983
Sally Ride becomes the first American woman in space.

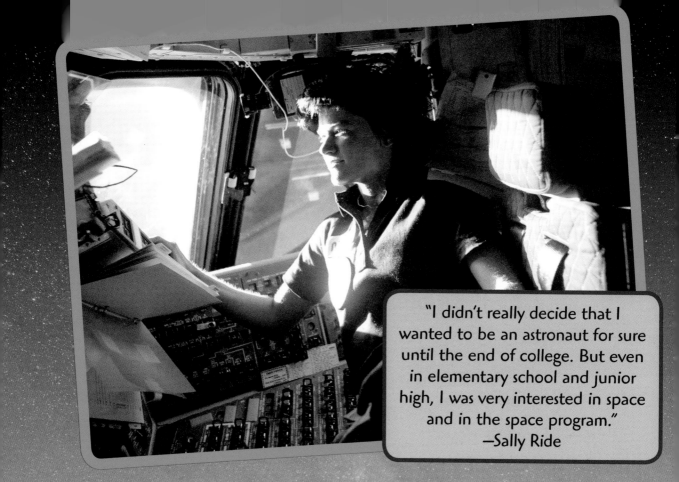

"I didn't really decide that I wanted to be an astronaut for sure until the end of college. But even in elementary school and junior high, I was very interested in space and in the space program."
—Sally Ride

1995
Eileen Collins is the first American woman to pilot a spacecraft.

1992
Mae Jemison becomes the first African-American woman in space.

1999
Eileen Collins is the first woman to command a U.S. space mission.

SPACE DISASTERS

The space shuttle program suffered two major disasters. The first came in 1986. On January 28, seven astronauts boarded *Challenger*. Just 73 seconds after liftoff, an explosion destroyed the shuttle. All seven astronauts died.

Challenger is destroyed during launch.

Another tragedy happened in 2003. The shuttle *Columbia* broke apart as it returned to Earth on February 1. All seven crew members died. After each disaster, NASA studied what went wrong. It made changes to make future space missions safer.

the crew of *Challenger*

the crew of *Columbia*

BRITONS IN SPACE

Astronaut Helen Sharman launched into space aboard a Soviet spacecraft in 1991. She became the first British citizen to travel into space. British companies helped pay for her trip. Sharman spent eight days on the Mir space station.

Helen Sharman

People born in the United Kingdom had flown into space before. However, they became U.S. citizens before flying with NASA.

The European Space Agency (ESA) trains astronauts from Europe to fly in space. The first British ESA astronaut was Tim Peake. He flew into space on December 15, 2015.

Tim Peake

FUTURE SPACE FLIGHTS

There are exciting missions ahead for NASA. The agency is building a new spacecraft called Orion. It will carry four astronauts into space. It may travel to the moon, to asteroids, or to Mars.

ORION
SPACECRAFT

Businesses are working on space travel too. SpaceX has a spacecraft called Dragon. Orbital ATK has one called Cygnus. Both have carried supplies to the ISS. These and other companies plan to make space flights easier and cheaper. More people will be able to go on space flights than ever before.

DRAGON SPACECRAFT

CYGNUS SPACECRAFT

GLOSSARY

asteroid—a rock that drifts through space

capsule—a small spacecraft that holds astronauts and other travelers

cosmonaut—a Russian astronaut

disaster—a sudden event that causes damage or loss of life

docking—connecting with another spacecraft in space

lander—a spacecraft designed to safely land on a moon or planet

orbit—the curved path of a spacecraft around an object in space

parachutist—a person who jumps out of airplanes with a parachute

spacewalk—leaving a spacecraft or space station to work outside

tether—a rope or cord that connects two objects together

tragedy—an event causing suffering and sadness

CRITICAL THINKING USING THE COMMON CORE

1. Where are some places that future space flights might go? (Key Ideas and Details)

2. How did the first U.S. space flight differ from the first Soviet space flight? (Key Ideas and Details)

3. Pages 16 and 17 discuss the first moon landing. Based on this description, would you want to walk on the moon, like Armstrong and Aldrin, or stay in the orbiting spacecraft, like Collins? (Integration of Knowledge and Ideas)

READ MORE

Bredeson, Carmen, and Marianne Dyson. *Astronauts Explore the Galaxy.* Launch into Space! New York: Enslow Publishing, 2015.

Green, Carl R. *Walking on the Moon: The Amazing Apollo 11 Mission.* American Space Missions—Astronauts, Exploration, and Discovery. Berkeley Heights, N.J.: Enslow Publishers, Inc., 2013.

Krumm, Brian. *Shuttle in the Sky: The Columbia Disaster.* Exploring Space and Beyond. North Mankato, Minn.: Capstone Press, 2016.

INTERNET SITES

FactHound offers a safe, fun way to find Internet sites related to this book. All of the sites on FactHound have been researched by our staff.

Here's all you do:

Visit www.facthound.com

Type in this code: 9781515736592

Check out projects, games and lots more at
www.capstonekids.com

INDEX